Gate Theatre presents, in association with Belvoir, Sydney

MEDEA

**By Kate Mulvany and Anne-Louise Sarks
After Euripides**

MEDEA

By Kate Mulvany and Anne-Louise Sarks
After Euripides

CAST

The roles of Jasper and Leon are played by alternating casts

In order of appearance

Jasper	**Samuel Menhinick**
Leon	**Bili Keogh**
Jasper	**Bobby Smalldridge**
Leon	**Keir Edkins-O'Brien**
Medea	**Emma Beattie**

Creative Team

Director	**Anne-Louise Sarks**
Designer	**Amy Jane Cook**
Lighting Designer	**Joshua Pharo**
Sound Designer	**Adrienne Quartly**
Production Manager	**Peter Williams**
Casting Director	**Debbie O'Brien**
Stage Manager	**Charlotte McBrearty**
Assistant Designer	**Lizzy Leech**
Assistant Director	**Bella Loudon**
Production Electrician	**Sarah Readman**
Chaperones	**Justin Kielty & Tanya Shields**
Press	**Kate Morley** for Kate Morley PR (kate@katemorleypr.com | 07970 465648)

The Gate would also like to thank the following people for their help with the development of this production: Helen Bauer, Jude Christian, Holly Gladwell, Jo Hawes, Ruth Hawkins, Lottie Hines, Helen Lynch, Elisabeth Morse, James Wilkinson, Kate O'Connor, Anastasia Osei-Kuffour, Jasmine Sandalli, Steve Sargeant, Anna Sheard, ikin yum, the team at Debbie O'Brien Casting, Brenna Hobson and the team at Belvoir, Sydney, the team at Theatre Delicatessen and the families of the cast.

MEDEA

CAST

SAMUEL MENHINICK – JASPER
Samuel trains at The Pauline Quirke Academy (Tonbridge) where his studies include Musical Theatre, Film & TV and Comedy & Drama.
Samuel's theatre credits include: *American Dreams* (Her Majesty's Theatre); *Fright Night* (Her Majesty's Theatre); *Priscilla Queen of the Desert* (UK Tour).
He has appeared in a Sainsbury commercial and a promo for Zinter 3D Printers.
Other work includes: *Puzzled* (Short Film); *Charlie and the Chocolate Factory* (Workshop); *Cinderella Rockerfella, Rock On & Star Paws* (EM Forster Theatre Tonbridge).

BILI KEOGH – LEON
Bili trains at Sylvia Young Theatre School.
He has appeared in the film *The Lady in the Van* and several commercials.

BOBBY SMALLDRIDGE – JASPER
Bobby's theatre credits include: *Oresteia* (Almeida Theatre); *God Bless the Child* (Royal Court Theatre); *Billy Elliot the Musical* (Victoria Palace Theatre, London).
Film credits include: *The Lost City of Z, What We Did on our Holiday, Foster*.
Television credits include: *Crossing Lines, Cockroaches, Harry and Paul's Story of the Two's, Casualty*, Robbie Williams *One Night at the London Palladium, Topsy and Time, Deadbeats, Miss Marple, What Shall We Do Today?, Kids Say the Funniest Things*. He has appeared in several commercials for companies including Alton Towers, Morrisons and Kellogg's.

KEIR EDKINS-O'BRIEN – LEON
Keir attends Reed's School and a theatre school on a Saturday and regularly attends Buttercup Agency drama workshops.
Keir's theatre credits include: *Charlie and the Chocolate Factory* (Theatre Royal Drury Lane); *Waiting for Godot* (Barbican). Keir also understudied the featured role of Sam and was also part of the chorus for the 800th celebration of the Magna Carta at the Royal Albert Hall. He has also performed at the Royal Opera House as part of the Olivier Awards 2014.
Keir's commercial credits include: B&Q and Sainsbury's. His other credits include the film *Abduct* and appearing in an online charity film against cruelty to animals.

EMMA BEATTIE – MEDEA
Emma trained at ALRA and was winner of the 1998 Lilian Baylis Award.
Theatre credits include: *The Distance* (Orange Tree Theatre); *The Odyssey* (Derby Playhouse); *The Last of the Haussmans* (National Theatre); *Death of a Cyclist* (Hotbed Festival – Soho Theatre); *Four for Jericho* (Pleasance Courtyard); *Great Expectations* (Watermill Theatre); The Song of Deborah (Lowry Theatre); *The Potting Shed* (Finborough Theatre); *Ivanov* (Wyndham's Theatre); *The Ruffian on the Stair* (Orange Tree Theatre); *John Gabriel Borkman* (Donmar Warehouse); *The Cut* (Donmar Warehouse); *King Lear* (Pendley Shakespeare Festival) and *Hysteria* (UK Tour).
Emma's screen credits include: *Catastrophe* (Channel 4); *The Wives Did it* (Discovery); *Mr Selfridge* (BBC); *Legacy* (Feature).

CREATIVE

AMY JANE COOK – DESIGNER
Amy trained at the Motley Theatre Design Course.

Theatre credits include: *The 8th* (UK tour/Paines Plough); *Mudlarks* (Bush/HighTide Festival); *65 Miles, Once Upon a Time in Wigan* (Hull Truck/Paines Plough); *Hamlet* (Young Vic/Maria Theatre); *66 Books, Flooded Grave, Where's My Seat?* (The Bush); *The Water Engine* (Old Vic Tunnels); *Almost, Maine* (The Park Theatre); *The Separation* (Project Arts Centre, Dublin/Theatre 503); *Thumbelina* (Cambridge Junction); *Space Junk* (The Lyric Studio); *Mydidae* (Trafalgar Studios/Soho Theatre); *Glory Dazed* (Soho Theatre); *The Mobile Phone Show* (The Lyric Studio); *Snow White* (The Old Vic & schools tour); *Where The Mangrove Grows* (Theatre 503); *I Heart Peterborough* (Pleasance Edinburgh/Soho Theatre); *The Pride* (Be Me Theatre, Munich); *A Midsummer Night's Dream* (Broadway Theatre); *W11* (The Gate Theatre, Notting Hill); *She Stoops to Conquer* (Hoxton Hall); *It's About Time* (Nabokov/Latitude); *Love's Labour's Lost* (Guildford Castle); *Limehouse Nights* (Limehouse Town Hall); *Ignite* (Complicité/Arts depot); *Manor* (Soho/Tristan Bates).

Film credits include: *Outside-In* (Take Cover Films); *Fred's Meat* (North London Film Awards).

www.amyjanecook.com

This role is funded by the Jerwood Charitable Foundation, as part of the Jerwood Young Designers Programme at the Gate.

LIZZY LEECH – ASSISTANT DESIGNER
Lizzy recently graduated from Bristol Old Vic Theatre School; prior to training she studied English Literature at Warwick University.

Recent designs include: *The Engineer's Corset* (Redgrave Theatre); *Allie* (Theatre Delicatessen and Guilded Balloon); *Treats* (Tobacco Factory); set for *Love for Love* (Bristol Old Vic); and costumes for *The Hersey of Love* (Bristol Old Vic). She also designed the sets for *Pornography* at the National Student Drama Festival 2013 and *RENT* at NSDF 2014. Recently she has assisted on *The Shawshank Redemption* (Bill Kenwright Ltd); *Crouch, Touch, Pause, Engage* (Out of Joint) and with the National Youth Theatre. Lizzy is very excited for her first time working at The Gate.

www.lizzyleech.com

This role is funded by the Jerwood Charitable Foundation, as part of the Jerwood Young Designers Programme at the Gate.

BELLA LOUDON – ASSISTANT DIRECTOR
Bella is the Co-founder and Artistic Director of In Tandem Theatre Company. She trained at Drama Centre London (BA Directing) in 2010-2013 and has been a Creative Associate at the Gate Theatre since 2014.

Since graduating she has directed work at: *Family Tree* (Theatre 503/Pleasance Courtyard Edinburgh); *My Parents Scratch (*Battersea Arts Centre); *Low Level Panic* (The Etcetera Theatre); *After Liverpool* (Rosemary Branch) and *Most People Are Other People* (Tristan Bates). She has also worked as an Associate Director for *Titus*

– UK tour (Macrobert); *Color Between The Lines* (Irondale Theatre NY); *Dead To Me* (Gary Kitching & co in association with Greyscale at Summerhall and UK Tour); and assisted on *Clean* & *A Respectable Widow Takes to Vulgarity* & *50 Plays for Edinburgh* (The Traverse Theatre / 59E59 NY); *Gods are Fallen and All Safety Gone* – UK tour (Greyscale Theatre Company); *I Promise You Sex and Violence* (Northern Stage) and *Gate Gala* & *I'd Rather Goya Robbed Me Of My Sleep Than Some Other Asshole* (The Gate Theatre, Notting Hill).

bellaloudon.wix.com/intandem

CHARLOTTE MCBREARTY – STAGE MANAGER

Charlotte trained at the Arts Institute at Bournemouth and is a Freelance Stage Manager who has worked all over the UK, and internationally. She has worked on productions that have received nominations for the Olivier Awards, and won Whatsonstage and Fringe First Awards. In the past year she has worked on productions with Paines Plough, Old Vic New Voices, DryWrite, Soho Theatre, Young Vic/Dance Umbrella, and Look Left Look Right. She is delighted to join The Gate for this production of *Medea*.

KATE MULVANY – WRITER

Kate Mulvany is an award-winning playwright, screenwriter and actor. Her most recent play, *Masquerade*, a reimagining of the much-loved children's book by Kit Williams, was performed at the 2015 Sydney Festival, the State Theatre Company of South Australia and the 2015 Melbourne Festival. Her autobiographical play *The Seed*, commissioned by Belvoir Street Theatre, won the Sydney Theatre Award for Best Independent Production. With Mulvany performing in the play, it received great critical success, toured nationally and is currently being developed into a feature film. She also recently adapted *Jasper Jones* from Craig Silvey's novel, which premièred for Barking Gecko Theatre Company in 2014 and will be seen at Belvoir and the Melbourne Theatre Company in 2016. In 2013 her play *The Rasputin Affair* was shortlisted for the Griffin New Play Award and for The Patrick White Award.

Other plays and musicals include: *The Danger Age* (Deckchair Theatre and La Boîte); *The Web* (Hothouse and Black Swan Theatre Company); *Somewhere* (co-written with Tim Minchin for the Joan Sutherland PAC) and *Storytime* (The Old Fitzroy Theatre) which won her the 2004 Philip Parsons Award. As an actor, Mulvany has performed most recently as Lady Macbeth in *Macbeth* and Cassius in *Julius Caesar* for Bell Shakespeare, and as Lucille McKee in Baz Luhrmann's *The Great Gatsby*. Kate is currently the Intersticia Fellow at Bell Shakespeare and the Patrick White Fellow at the Sydney Theatre Company.

DEBBIE O'BRIEN – CASTING DIRECTOR

West End productions include: *American Idiot*, *Dusty*, *Thriller Live*, *The Bodyguard* and *Kinky Boots* (children's casting); *Priscilla Queen of the Desert*, *Grease*, *Flashdance*, *Piaf*, *The Snowman*, *Respect La Diva*, *The King and I*, *The Harder They Come*, *Showboat*, *Dancing in the Streets*, *The Rat Pack Live from Las Vegas*, *Chitty Chitty Bang Bang*, *Saturday Night Fever*, *Fame*, *Peter Pan*, *The Pirates of Penzance*, *Mum's the Word*, *Daisy Pulls It Off*, *Napoleon*, *Hedwig and the Angry Inch*, *La Cava*, *Smokey Joe's Café*, *The Rocky Horror Show*, *Soul Train*.

UK tours include: *Dirty Dancing, Annie* (children's casting); *The Threepenny Opera, Our House, Soul Sister, I Was a Rat, Carnaby Street, 51 Shades of Maggie, Doctor In the House, Hormonal Housewives, Grease, Tell Me On a Sunday, Cacophony, Menopause the Musical, Mahabharata, Sweet Soul Music, Starlight Express, Anything Goes, What a Feeling, A Chorus Line, A Tribute to the Blues Brothers, Smokey Joe's Cafe, The Rocky Horror Show, Soul Train, Wild Animus.*

Regional and international productions include: *Sweet Charity, Singing in the Rain, Legally Blonde, Cougar, Cats* (RCCL); *Midsummer Songs, The BFG, South Pacific, Sister Act, Much Ado About Nothing, As You Like It, A Midsummer Night's Dream, Romeo and Juliet, The Comedy of Errors, Merry Wives of Windsor and Twelfth Night, Jackie the Musical, Hairspray, Starlight Express* (Bochum and international tour); *Fame, Alice In Wonderland, The Sound of Music.*

Recorded media: *Waybuloo, Grandpa In My Pocket, What's Your News?, Buddy Patrol, Tic Toc, Quick Quack Duck, Planet Cook, Energy.*

JOSHUA PHARO – LIGHTING DESIGNER

Joshua works as a Lighting and Projection Designer across theatre, dance, opera, music, film & art installation.

Current projects include: *Glass Menagerie* (Nuffield Theatre) as Video Designer; *Invisible Treasure* (Ovalhouse Theatre); *The Merchant of Venice, Wuthering Heights, Consensual* (Ambassadors Theatre); *The Crocodile* (Manchester International Festival); *One Arm* (Southwark Playhouse); *The Trial Parallel* (Young Vic); *Amadis de Gaulle* (Bloomsbury Theatre); *Beckett Season* (Old Red Lion); *The Deluge* (UK Tour, Lila Dance); *Usagi Yojimbo* (Southwark Playhouse); *A Streetcar Named Desire Parallel* (Young Vic); *Trace Elements* (UK Tour, Janine Fletcher); *Werther* (Arcola); *Be Here Now* (Shoreditch Town Hall, TOOT); *Pioneer* (UK Tour, Curious Directive); *I'd Rather Goya Robbed Me of My Sleep* (The Gate Theatre, Notting Hill); *Thumbelina* (UK Tour, Dancing Brick); *No Place Like Home* (TheGate); *Pelleas et Melisande* (Arcola & Bury Court).

Recent video & lighting credits include: *Mikvah Project* (Yard Theatre); *Nicobobinus* (UK Tour, Red Ladder); *Fox Symphony* (Camden People's Theatre, Foxy & Husk); *The Hundred We Are* (Yard Theatre, Hobo Theatre); *Brothers of Justice* (Camden People's Theatre).

Recent video credits include: *The Hook* (Royal and Derngate Theatre and Liverpool Playhouse) as Associate Video Designer; *The Curious Incident of a Dog in the Night Time* (Gielgud) as Associate Video Designer.

More info at: www.joshuapharo.com

ADRIENNE QUARTLY – SOUND DESIGNER

Adrienne is a freelance sound designer and composer. She trained at RCSSD, London.

Previous shows include: *Splendour*, (Donmar Warehouse); *Bad Jews* (Arts, London); *Ghost Train* (Royal Exchange, Manchester); *The Whipping Man* (TRP, Plymouth); *The Ladykillers* (Watermill); *Sex & 3 day week* (Liverpool Playhouse); *Inside Wagner's Head* (Royal Opera House); *Grand Guignol*, (Southwark); *Juvenalia* (Assembly, Edinburgh); *Every Last Trick* (Spymonkey); *Untold Stories* (West Yorkshire Playhouse); *I'd Rather Goya Robbed Me of My Sleep Than Some Other Arsehole* (The Gate Theatre, Notting Hill); *Tale of Two Cities, Body of an American* (Royal & Derngate, Northampton); *After Electra* (Tricycle Theatre) *Get*

MEDEA

Happy, And the Horse, Fräulein Julie (Barbican); *Too Clever, You Can't Take It With You* (Royal Exchange); *Merit* (Theatre Royal Plymouth); *Chekov in Hell* (Soho Theatre); *The Astronaut's Chair, Horse Piss for Blood, Nostalgia* (Theatre Royal Plymouth); *The Shawl, The Container* (Young Vic); *The Vortex* (Rose Theatre, Kingston); *The Importance of Being Earnest* (Hong Kong Arts Festival); *Three Little Pigs* (Circo Ridiculoso); *One Monkey* (Eclipse); *Rings of Saturn* (Cologne); *The Roundabout (*Paines Plough); *Stockholm* (Frantic Assembly); *Thomas Hobbes* (Royal Shakespeare Company); *365* (National Theatre Scotland); *Woyzeck* (St Ann's, NYC); *The Painter* (Arcola Theatre); *Reykjavik* (Roundhouse); *93.2FM* (Royal Court); *The Fastest Clock* (Hampstead Theatre); *Faustus, School for Scandal, Volpone, The Duchess of Malfi* (Stage on Screen).

www.adriennequartly.com

ANNE-LOUISE SARKS – DIRECTOR

Anne-Louise is currently Resident Director at Belvoir in Sydney, Australia. From 2010 to 2013 she was Artistic Director of The Hayloft Project. She was previously a director-in-residence at Malthouse Theatre in Melbourne. Anne-Louise has worked professionally as a director, playwright, actor and dramaturge with Australia's most highly regarded theatre companies including Belvoir, The Malthouse Theatre in Melbourne, and Melbourne Theatre Company.

For Belvoir Anne-Louise has directed *Stories I Want to Tell You in Person* and *Seventeen*, she co-wrote and directed *Nora* and *Medea*, *Elektra/Orestes* and *A Christmas Carol*. Anne-Louise was assistant director on Simon Stone's *The Wild Duck*, and dramaturg on Posts' *Oedipus Schmoedipus*, Sisters Grimm's *La Traviata* and The Hayloft Project's *Thyestes*.

Medea won five Sydney Theatre Awards including Best Direction, Best Mainstage Production and Best New Australian Work. It was also awarded an AWGIE for Best Stage Play and nominated for four 2013 Helpmann Awards including Best Direction, Best New Australian Work and Best Play.

Anne-Louise's other theatre credits include: *The Seed* (Melbourne Theatre Company); *The Nest, Yuri Wells* and *By Their Own Hands* (The Hayloft Project).
Her acting credits include: *The Suicide, By Their Own Hands* (B Sharp/ The Hayloft Project/Neon MTC); *3XSisters, The Only Child* (The Hayloft Project, Best Independent Production, Sydney Theatre Awards); *Return to Earth* (Melbourne Theatre Company); *The Spook* (Malthouse Theatre); and *Starchaser* (Arena Theatre Company).

PETER WILLIAMS – PRODUCTION MANAGER

Pete has worked in Technical theatre for nearly 30 years which has taken him all over the world including off Broadway, working for companies such Backrow Productions, Vanessa Ford Productions, Seabright Productions & the RSC.

These days he works more on large events including 3 Olympic events – London 2012, Sochi 2012 & Azerbaijan 2015 – in various Technical roles & is more than likely heading to Rio 2016.

This is the third show Peter has production managed for the Gate which also include *The Sexual Neuroses Of Our Parents* & *Car Cemetery*. He is very pleased to be back doing *Medea*.

The Gate is committed to being environmentally responsible. In line with our Green Gate policy, these playtexts are printed on FSC certified paper.

If you're finished with it, why not donate this book to a charity shop, or recycle where possible?

To find out more about our Green Gate policy, please visit www.gatetheatre.co.uk

MEDEA

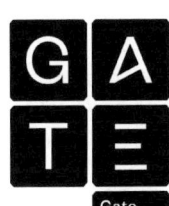

Gate Theatre Notting Hill

About the Gate Theatre
'London's most relentlessly ambitious theatre'
Time Out

The Gate sits above the Prince Albert pub in Notting Hill, and has been inspiring audiences and artists alike for 35 years. We are a small theatre but we always Think Big.

We are a home for anarchic spirits, invigorating theatre, and restless creative ambition. We welcome anyone who wants to change the world. In our ever transformable, 75 seat space we confront and debate the biggest questions that face humanity and act as a loudspeaker for unheard voices from across the globe. We are known to springboard the most exceptional new talent into becoming the theatre leaders of tomorrow. No two visits to the Gate are ever the same.

Artistic Director **Christopher Haydon**

Executive Director **Clare Slater**

Associate Director* **Tinuke Craig**

Producer **Daisy Cooper**

General Manager **Chrissy Angus**

Development Manager **Fiona English**

Technical Manager* **Andrew Rungen**

Finance Manager **Jo Hawkes**
(maternity cover)*

Marketing and Audience Development Officer **Natasha Brown**

Administrator **Suzy Sancho**

Development Intern **Bobette Kenge**

*Indicates part-time role

Front of House **Rike Berge, Chiara Ciabattoni, Pippa Davis, Hannah Forrester, Chloe France, Eloise Green, Nick Hafezi, Esther Huntington, Susan Keats, Zoe Lambraskis, Kieran Lucas, Alasdair MacLeod, Katy Munroe Farlie, Cecily Rabley, Eleanor Rose, Annabel Williamson, James York, Naomi Wright**

Associate Artists **Rachel Chavkin, Lucy Ellinson, Ellen McDougall, Clare Slater, Oliver Townsend, Charlotte Westenra**

Creative Associates **Daisy Bunyan, Caroline Byrne, Jude Christian, Amy Draper, Ela Brunel Hawes, Rebecca Hill, Petra Hjortsberg, Zoe Hurwitz, Magdalena Iwanska, Maria Koutsouna, Lizzy Leech, Anna Lewis, Lynette Linton, Bella Loudon, Sophie Moniram, Anastasia Osei-Kuffour, Kate O'Connor, Alasdair Pidsley, Melanie Spencer, Anne Reid, Tara Robson, Jennifer Tang, Benjamin Walden**

The Gate Theatre Board of Trustees **Joseph Smith** (Chair), **Sian Alexander, Natasha Bucknor, Sarah Chappatte Lang, Lauren Clancy, Kobna Holdbrook-Smith, David Lakhdhir, Nicole Newman, Charles Prideaux, Mark Robinson, Colin Simon**

Development Working Group **Teresa Alpert, Sarah Chappatte Lang, Lauren Clancy, Charles Cormick, Richard Grandison, Linda Lakhdhir, Rita Laven, Anne Marie Mackay, Kate Maltby, Nicole Newman, Barbara Prideaux, Mark Robinson, Joseph Smith**

The Gate Theatre Company is a company limited by guarantee.
Registered in England & Wales No. 1495543 | Charity No. 280278
Registered address: 11 Pembridge Road, Above the Prince Albert Pub, London, W11 3HQ

The Gate has been inspiring audiences and artists alike for 35 years. Thanks to our Supporters, we are able to keep telling challenging, inspirational stories, in an intimate space, on an epic scale.

Our Supporters are invited behind the scenes to discover more about the performances and are given the unique chance to meet and engage with the theatre leaders of tomorrow.

Please join us as a Supporter to celebrate the most exceptional new talent whilst helping to ensure we are around for the next 35 years. Join us and change the world.
gatetheatre.co.uk

To join as a Gate Supporter from £250 a year, please contact

Fiona English, Development Manager
fiona@gatetheatre.co.uk
020 7229 5387

The Gate Theatre is a registered charity (No. 280278)

MEDEA

The Gate would like to thank the following for their continued generous support:

GATE GUARDIANS Katrina and Chris Barter, Tim and Amy Bevan, Geraldine and Chris Brodie, Lauren and Michael Clancy, Leslie Feeney, Richard and Jan Grandison, James Hughes-Hallett, Helen and Paul Jameson, Addy Loudiadis, Kate Maltby, Miles Morland, Nicola and James Reed, Jon and NoraLee Sedmak, The Emmanuel Kaye Foundation.

GATE AMBASSADORS Arianne Braillard and Francesco Cincotta, Caroline and Jim Clark, Nick and Jane Ferguson, Penny and Barry Francis, Thomas and Julie Hoegh, David and Abigail Lacey, David and Linda Lakhdhir, Georgia Oetker, Ellen and Michel Plantevin, Charles and Barbara Prideaux, Scott Stevens and Eva Boenders, Jan Topham, The Ulrich Family, Bill and Anda Winters.

GATE KEEPERS Tina and Habib Achkar, The Agency (London) Ltd., Matthew Bannister, Paula Marie Black, Christiane and Bruno Boesch, Neil and Sarah Brener, Sarah and Phillippe Chappatte, Charles Cormick, Robert Devereux, David Emmerson, Joachim Fleury, Tony Mackintosh, Andy McIntyre, Alan and Jan Morgan, Elisabeth Morse, Lyndsey Posner, Mark and Claire Ralf, Pascale Revert and Peter Wheeler, Mark Robinson, David and Susie Sainsbury, Paul and Caroline Weiland.

GATE YOUNG SUPPORTERS NETWORK Ella Kaye, Kate Maltby.
Thank you to all our Gate Openers, Gate New Plays Fund and Directors' Appeal supporters too.

TRUSTS AND FOUNDATIONS Arts Council England, Backstage Trust, Fidelio, Garrick Charitable Trust, Jerwood Charitable Foundation, Royal Borough of Kensington & Chelsea, The Emmanuel Kaye Foundation, The Fenton Arts Trust, The Goldsmiths' Company, The Mercers' Company and the Wates Foundation.

CORPORATE SUPPORTERS The Shed Restaurant, Rien Qui Bouge, Polpo Notting Hill

Special thanks to Jenny Hall

Jerwood Young Designers

Since 2001 Jerwood Young Designers has given outstanding individuals in the opportunity to lead on the design of the productions at the Gate Theatre in Notting Hill. In 2013, acknowledging the creative ambition of the Gate's productions, this programme grew to include support for design assistants.

The Gate has long had a reputation as one of the most versatile studio spaces in London, perfect for designers to explore theatrical possibilities. They also have the chance to work with some of the finest directors and writers working in theatre, an experience which is invaluable in establishing reputation and contacts.

The support that the Jerwood Young Designers Programme provides in both nurturing talent and offering the opportunity of practical experience has been instrumental in launching the careers of some of the country's most exciting theatrical designers.

By the end of the 2015/16 programme, Jerwood will have supported 76 placements on the Young Designers Programme over the course of 14 years.

www.jerwoodcharitablefoundation.org

Medea was first produced by Belvoir Street Theatre, at the Downstairs Theatre on 13 October 2012, with the following cast:

MEDEA	**Blazey Best**
LEON	**Joseph Kelly**
JASPER	**Rory Potter**
WRITERS	**Kate Mulvany and Anne-Louise Sarks**
DIRECTOR	**Anne-Louise Sarks**
SET & COSTUME DESIGN	**Mel Page**
LIGHTING DESIGN	**Benjamin Cisterne**
COMPOSER & SOUND DESIGN	**Stefan Gregory**
ASSISTANT DIRECTOR	**Laura Turner**
STAGE MANAGER	**Kelly Ukena**
ASSISTANT STAGE MANAGER	**Grace Nye-Butler**

With thanks to the Australian Theatre for Young People for having helped develop the play.

Introductions from the Writers

It's always terrifying to be asked to 'adapt'. What, after all, does that really mean? How tight or loose are the boundaries? How much of ourselves are we allowed, as creators, to infiltrate the text? How do we take a classic – with all its potency, its history, its collective memory – and make it our own whilst keeping the purity of the original?

These are the questions I had to ask myself when I was approached to adapt Medea with Anne-Louise Sarks. Two women retelling the story of the most infamous mother in history. Or rather, in our case, telling the story of Medea's children – so absent in other retellings and yet the two souls on which the story hinges.

And this was the key to exploding our adaptive boundaries. Those forgotten children. Those two little boys in the midst of a marital maelstrom.

This subverted version of Medea was written after an intensive two-week workshop with two boys – Joe Kelly and Rory Potter - aged 12 and 11. I am indebted to them.

Many of the moments in this play came about through their own invention, such as particular songs, lines and even their names. ('Leon' means 'brave warrior' and 'Jasper' means 'precious stone'.)

Part of the joy of bringing this text to life was that freedom of choice from the boys – a freedom that made my initial concerns about adapting a classic null and void. They took the story and made it their own anyway. They had no notion of 'textual purity'. They just wanted to tell their story. And this writer followed their belligerent path happily.

To me, the play you are about to read is still Medea at heart, but for the first time ever we get to hear the children speak. We get to see them play. We get to see them laugh and tease and cry and examine their own existence. More importantly, we get to spend their last hour on earth with them when no-one else in history has.

And that's why I'm so happy we busted the boundaries of 'adaptation'. My eternal thanks to Annie-Lou for inviting us into the playground.

Kate Mulvany

MEDEA

The process of creating any new work is a series of what ifs.

This ongoing questioning gives birth to even more what ifs – that are then shaped into a living, breathing experience. And finally an audience comes to participate in the collective what if.

What if this myth was real?

What if I was heartbroken? What if I had two children and believed I would lose them forever? What if I was an outsider with no one to turn to? Or what if Mum was upset and being really weird? What if I was locked in my room all day and I needed to wee?

This Medea began its life inside of me as a bold and persistent what if – in terms of the story of Medea, but also in terms of what is possible in the theatre with children. I believe children bring an electricity to the stage. They change the quality of the air with their playfulness and their truth. In this new Medea that electricity is at the centre of the theatrical experience.

The story of Medea is not some distant mythic tale that bears no relationship to life today. There are too many recent stories of parents taking the lives of their own children for us to dismiss its relevance. The horrific story of Darcey Freeman being thrown off Melbourne's West Gate Bridge by her father in January 2009 is only one such story, but it stayed with me. When I later learned that Darcey's brother Ben, then six years old, had said to his father, "Go back and get her. Darcey can't swim.", I was overwhelmed. There was something about the heart-breaking combination of his knowledge and his naivety that struck me. It completely changed the way I saw that terrible act.

How does a child see the world? And how do they understand such epic events? What if I tried to tell the story of a tragedy through the eyes of that child?

This play was made originally for Belvoir's downstairs theatre. Kate Mulvany and I began with the myth of Medea as a loose framework for the new work, but very quickly our piece became more than the offstage reality of the original Medea. It became a world all of its own.

Since then it has had a life in Warsaw, and now I'm delighted to be reimagining it for the Gate Theatre.

Our initial script was devised by the original artists involved and was shaped by their voices. I'm incredibly grateful to all those involved for their openness and generosity.

Everyone embraced the unusual process and celebrated the obstacles that such a process demanded, none more so than the two talented young actors who first brought Medea's boys to life, Joe Kelly and Rory Potter.

Now here in London a team of incredibly talented artists are bringing this world to life in a completely new way. They are imbuing our original what ifs with their own instincts and playfulness.

I have had to teach these young actors about the process of theatre, about theatre's language and its strange rituals, but they have taught me more. They have given me the precious gift of seeing again – because they are children, thus far only partially formed by the forces that shape us all, but also because they are their own individuals, with their individual ways of seeing.

They have helped me to see the world of Medea and the Greeks again, as well as the world we all live in. But most significantly, they have given me the pleasure of seeing anew this world of theatre that I love. For that I am eternally grateful.

Anne-Louise Sarks

MEDEA

Kate Mulvany and Anne-Louise Sarks
after Euripides

MEDEA

A new adaptation of the Greek myth

Original concept by Anne-Louise Sarks for Belvoir

OBERON BOOKS
LONDON

WWW.OBERONBOOKS.COM

First published in 2012 by Playlab, as part of *Downstairs at Belvoir*

This edition first published in 2015 by Oberon Books Ltd
521 Caledonian Road, London N7 9RH
Tel: +44 (0) 20 7607 3637 / Fax: +44 (0) 20 7607 3629
e-mail: info@oberonbooks.com
www.oberonbooks.com

Copyright © Kate Mulvany and Anne-Louise Sarks, 2015

Kate Mulvany and Anne-Louise Sarks are hereby identified as authors of this play in accordance with section 77 of the Copyright, Designs and Patents Act 1988. The authors have asserted their moral rights.

All rights whatsoever in this play are strictly reserved and application for performance etc. should be made before commencement of rehearsal to Cameron's Management (info@cameronsmanagement.com.au). No performance may be given unless a licence has been obtained, and no alterations may be made in the title or the text of the play without the author's prior written consent.

You may not copy, store, distribute, transmit, reproduce or otherwise make available this publication (or any part of it) in any form, or binding or by any means (print, electronic, digital, optical, mechanical, photocopying, recording or otherwise), without the prior written permission of the publisher. Any person who does any unauthorized act in relation to this publication may be liable to criminal prosecution and civil claims for damages.

A catalogue record for this book is available from the British Library.

PB ISBN: 9781783193035
E ISBN: 9781783193042

Cover image by The Champion Agency

Printed and bound by 4edge Limited, UK.
eBook conversion by CPI Group (UK) Ltd, Croydon, CR0 4YY.

Visit www.oberonbooks.com to read more about all our books and to buy them. You will also find features, author interviews and news of any author events, and you can sign up for e-newsletters so that you're always first to hear about our new releases.

NOTE FROM CO-CREATORS:

This play was written after an intensive two-week workshop with two boys aged 12 and 11. We are indebted to them.

Many of the moments in this play came about through their own invention, such as particular songs, lines and even their names. ('Leon' means 'brave warrior' and 'Jasper' means 'precious stone'.)

Part of the joy of bringing this text to life, we believe, is that freedom of choice from the children, so we have highlighted moments in the script where we encourage the creatives to trust in the imaginations of their young cast. We have articulated this in the stage directions.

Because this play is written for two young actors, we have used quite descriptive and (occasionally!) prescriptive stage directions to ensure safety, understanding and distinct storytelling. Use as you see fit.

Have fun!

Kate Mulvany and Anne-Louise Sarks

1

Two boys, JASPER and LEON, lay perfectly still – dead? – on the floor of their messy bedroom. There are toys littered all over the place.

Hundreds of luminescent stars are stuck to the wall, but for now, they are unobtrusive in the light room.

Two fish swim in a fishbowl.

A long time passes.

A very long time.

Even longer …

Longer.

Then …

JASPER raises his head and glances at LEON.

LEON doesn't move.

JASPER puts his head back down.

He raises his head again and peers at LEON.

Nothing.

Puts his head back down.

JASPER gets up and goes to LEON.

JASPER: Leon.

LEON doesn't move.

JASPER pokes LEON.

LEON doesn't move.

JASPER pokes LEON again.

LEON stays still.

JASPER gets up and tries to wake LEON up. He uses various methods.

He pokes him again.

Nothing.

He makes LEON wipe his own bottom.

Nothing.

He rolls LEON over.

Nothing.

He drags LEON across the floor by his arms.

Nothing.

He makes LEON pick his nose and eat it.

Nothing.

JASPER: Hey.

Nothing.

Nincompoop.

Nothing.

He brings up a glob of throat snot. Threatens to spit on LEON.

Nothing.

He hovers his bottom over LEON's face.

I'll fart in your face. I will.

He strains.

LEON doesn't move.

Leon.

LEON doesn't move.

LEON!

Nothing.

Leon, wake up. Stop it.

Nothing.

Leon, that's enough!

Nothing.

Leon, if you don't get up, I'm gonna tell Mum.

Nothing. JASPER calls to the door.

Mum!

Nothing. JASPER calls out again.

MUM!

Nothing.

LEON! STOP IT! I'M ONLY LITTLE! MUM!

He tries open the door. It's locked. JASPER goes to his bed and sulks.

2

LEON suddenly leaps up and grabs his toy gun. He starts shooting JASPER.

JASPER screams, then grabs his own gun and fights back. The fight goes on for some time, with foam bullets flying around the space.

(Don't worry about hitting the audience – remember, they are not there. They may react, but just keep fighting. The bullets won't hurt them. Keep fighting, long and as loud. Have fun.)

After awhile, LEON 'dies' an incredibly graphic and impressive death as JASPER watches on. When LEON is on the ground and has been dead for awhile …

JASPER: That was awesome.

LEON wakes up.

My turn.

LEON: OK.

LEON prepares his weapon.

JASPER: No bullets required.

JASPER grabs a nearby bow and arrow and looks around dramatically. Puts on another voice.

'There's danger in these here hills' –

Suddenly, in his normal voice –

Oh, wait. I didn't tell you my back story.

LEON: You don't need a back story. Just die, Jasper.

JASPER: I'm a hunter and I've just come across a rabid bear in the forest and it's about to attack. Quick, throw Hercules at me.

LEON: It's better with bullets.

JASPER: Throw Hercules after I've said my line.

LEON picks up the teddy bear (Hercules). JASPER puts on his voice again.

JASPER: 'There's danger in these here hills' –

LEON throws the teddy bear at JASPER who does his Best Death as Hercules 'attacks' him. It's graphic and impressive.

LEON: OK, my turn again. I'm gonna die on my bed so I'm comfortable.

JASPER: Back story?

LEON: An arrow pierces my cerebral cortex, which results in … a MASSIVE SEIZURE!!!

He has a massive seizure then dies a Best Death.

JASPER drops to the floor too. They both play dead.

They play dead for ages.

Longer …

After a VERY long time.

JASPER: You opened your eyes. I win.

LEON: You had your eyes open!

JASPER: Did not!

LEON: Then how do you know my eyes were open?

Beat. JASPER has no answer for that. He's been caught out. He sits down crossly.

LEON sits on his bed. He plays with a badminton racquet and a shuttlecock. Hits it rhythmically over and over.

JASPER tries the door. It's locked.

He sits down crossly again.

3

Stillness. Silence. Bored.

Really, really bored.

JASPER checks the door. It's locked.

JASPER: I'm BORED. How long do we have to stay in here?

LEON: Till Mum and Dad have sorted stuff out.

JASPER: What stuff?

LEON: Marriage stuff. Love.

JASPER: Love. That's gross.

Beat.

She didn't have to lock the door. What if Mr Whippy drives past?

LEON: He doesn't come on (insert relevant day here).

JASPER: What if I need to wee?

LEON: You'll just have to cross your legs and not think about it.

A beat.

JASPER is already thinking about weeing. He shifts uncomfortably.

JASPER: How long does marriage stuff take to sort out?

LEON: Depends.

JASPER: On what?

LEON: On if they still love each other or not.

JASPER: So does it take longer if they do love each other or if they don't?

LEON: Well, it probably takes longer if they don't love each other.

JASPER: Why?

LEON: Because if they do love each other, it only takes a kiss to make up. If they don't love each other, they have to work out where it all went wrong and that could take at least an hour.

JASPER: Luckily Mum and Dad love each other.

LEON: I reckon.

JASPER: So they can kiss and make up and then we can go outside.

LEON: Yes.

JASPER: Sometimes their kisses take forever though. Once I timed them. I got to seventy-four.

LEON: You're weird.

JASPER: I'm just saying, sometimes a kiss lasts a really long time. So we could be stuck in here for awhile.

Silence.

More boredom.

LEON keeps playing with the shuttlecock. He looks at the fish in the bowl – Cornelius and Jay Jr. (You may call the fish whatever you like.)

LEON: Have you fed Cornelius and Jay Jr?

JASPER: It's not my turn.

LEON: I did it yesterday. Therefore, it is indeed your turn.

JASPER rolls his eyes and goes to the fish. Feeds them.
Not too much, Jasper. They'll explode.

JASPER: Awesome.

He feeds them heaps more.

LEON: Jasper!

LEON snatches the food away from JASPER.

Dad brought those fish all the way back from the Far East. They cost $100. EACH. So don't explode them.

LEON goes back to his bed and lays on it. Bored.

JASPER talks to the fish.

JASPER: Do you speak Chinese? Do you? Konichiwa?

He watches the fish intently. Then …

He shifts his gaze to the lock of the door.

Tries to open it with his mind.

Through magic.

Mind magic.

Nothing.

They both lay in the space, bored.

After awhile …

JASPER: Pig.

LEON doesn't hear.

Hey! Pig!

LEON plays the game.

LEON: Oh. Gecko.

JASPER: Orangutan.

LEON: Gorilla.

JASPER: Echidna … no! Echidna starts with an E. A? Ah … amore … armadillo!

LEON: Ostrich.

A beat. JASPER is struggling to find an answer.

While we're still young.

JASPER: Humpback whale.

LEON: Elephant.

JASPER: Echidna. Yeah!

LEON: Elephant ends with a t, idiot.

JASPER: I got mixed up. Turtle.

LEON: Echidna.

JASPER: I totally gave you that. Ant.

LEON: T-rex.

JASPER: That's not an animal. It's extinct. Ant!

LEON: Just because it ceases to exist doesn't mean it wasn't an animal. Tyrannosaurus means 'tyrant lizard'. A lizard is an animal. Therefore, so is a tyrannosaurus. Touché.

JASPER: It's dead! Dead things don't count.

LEON: Fine. Toucan.

JASPER: N … n … na … na … banana … Na … gnashing teeth … Norway … Norway … that's a country … Narwhal!

LEON: What the hell is a narwhal? You made that up.

JASPER: A narwhal is a cross between a unicorn and a whale.

LEON: Oh, so I can't use tyrannosaurus, but you can use unicorn?

JASPER: Unicorns aren't extinct!

LEON: That's cos they don't even exist!

JASPER: Then how do you explain narwhals then? Huh?

LEON looks confused.

Exactly. I win.

LEON rummages under his pillow and gets out some headphones and an MP3. He makes a show of putting on his headphones and listening to music. After all, JASPER is not yet old enough for headphones.

JASPER rolls his eyes.

JASPER: Teenagers.

4

JASPER goes to the fish bowl.

After a little while, he speaks to Cornelius and Jay Jr.

Would you two like to hear a story?

He mimes the fish speaking.

'Yes, please.'

He speaks to LEON.

Tell the story, Leon!

LEON ignores him.

Leon! Your fish would like to hear the story.

Nothing. LEON keeps listening to his music.

(To CORNELIUS.) Cornelius, I'm afraid you have a terrible parent. You can eavesdrop while I tell Jay Jr the story. I don't mind.

He clears his throat.

Once upon a time there was a brave and handsome man called … Dad.

Dad wanted this thing called the Golden Fleece …

Beat.

Leon! Why did Dad want a sheepskin?

LEON: Cos it's golden. And if you have it, you live forever. Apparently.

JASPER: Cool. And Dad had to go to a faraway island to get it. So he took some of his mates on a boat called …
Leon! What was the boat called again?

LEON: The Argo.

JASPER: The Argo. And from that time on, Dad and his merry men were known as …
Leon! What were they called again?

LEON: The Argonauts.

JASPER: The Argonauts. And one day they came to this deserted island where the Golden Fleece was protected by a huge army.

LEON: This story is boring, Jasper.

JASPER: No, it's not. It's **OUR** story!

LEON: OK. So then the Argonauts were in deep shit.

JASPER: Um-ah.

LEON: I said SHIP. The Argonauts were in a deep SHIP. And Mum lived on the island too. And she said, 'I will tell you how to conquer the army if you promise to take me away from this land and make me your wife.' Cos she hated where she lived.

JASPER: Why?

LEON: She didn't get on with her Dad.

JASPER: Why not?

LEON: She was naughty.

JASPER: What'd she do?

LEON: She never says. But I reckon it was pretty bad.

JASPER: Did she break something of Granddad's?

LEON: Worse, I reckon.

JASPER: Did she smoke a cigarette?

LEON: I reckon it was even worse than smoking.

JASPER: Wow. And she loved Dad. She wanted to be with him.

LEON: She hated where she lived AND she loved Dad.

JASPER: And he loved her. So it was a win-win.

LEON: And Mum said, 'I will tell you how to conquer the army if you promise to take me away from this land and make me your wife.'

JASPER: 'Because I love you, darling.'

LEON: 'Because I love you, darling.'

JASPER: And then Dad said, "I love you too and of course I'll take you back with me, sweetheart." And so Mum helped Dad and the Arthurnauts get the Golden Fleece and he took Mum back with him to his home because they loved each other and they became really famous and they had two kids – me and you.

A beat.

And where do our fish come into it?

LEON: Dad brought the fish back from his adventures.

Beat.

So don't explode them.

JASPER talks to the fish.

JASPER: How do you two live under water like that?

LEON: They hold their breath. Try it. I'll tell you when you can breathe.

JASPER holds his breath. LEON watches intently, enjoying the silence. JASPER turns very red.

Suddenly –

Did you hear that?

JASPER: What?

LEON: I think Dad's here!

The boys run to the door and try to hear. They cannot. LEON hurries to his bedside table where there is a glass of water. He pours the water into the fishbowl and places the glass against the door. He listens.

JASPER: Is it Dad?

LEON: Shh!

Beat.

JASPER: Is it Dad?

LEON: Shh!

Beat.

JASPER: Leon, is it Dad?

LEON: Shut up, Jasper!

A long moment as LEON listens. Really long. JASPER tries to grab the glass a few times. LEON is too tall for him. JASPER tries everything he can to get the glass. He stands on tiptoes. He climbs on LEON who shoves him away. He builds a mountain of toys to stand on. Whatever might get him taller, he tries to do. But he just can't get tall enough to reach the glass. Besides, LEON won't let him.

JASPER: What are they saying? Are they fighting?

LEON keeps listening.

LEON!

LEON keeps listening as he holds JASPER at bay. Then … his face shifts. He slides the glass from the wall and gives it to JASPER who listens through it. As he does, LEON gets Hercules, blindfolds him and places him against the wall.

JASPER: What's that noise?

A long silence as he listens through the glass.

I can't hear Dad.

Did he go?

Leon, did Dad go without seeing us?

LEON is still setting up Hercules.

JASPER listens through the glass some more. A long moment …

Is that …

Is that Mum?

LEON tortures Hercules. JASPER keeps listening.

Why is she crying?

LEON tortures Hercules some more. More listening from JASPER.

Do you reckon she's hurt herself?

LEON keeps torturing Hercules.

Hey … do you reckon she's hurt herself?

LEON tortures the bear over and over and over.

JASPER keeps listening through the glass. A long moment of listening.

Well, she's going to hurt herself if she keeps crying like that. Her throat. You know when you yell really loud and your throat starts to hurt? That's what's going to happen to her.

> *A beat.*

> *Then …*

> *LEON yells long and loud as he slaughters Hercules.*

LEON:
AAAAAAAAAAAAAAAARRRRRGGGGHHHHHHH!!!!

> *JASPER joins in.*

JASPER:
AAAAAAAAAAAAAAAARRRRRRGGGHHHHHHHH!!!

> *Both boys scream and scream and scream. It feels really good.*

BOTH:
AAAAAAAAAARRRRRRGGGGGHHHHH!!!!!!!!!!!!!!!!

5

The door suddenly flies open. It is MEDEA. She wears men's tracksuit pants, t-shirt and glittering jewellery. Her hair has been styled, but it is rapidly coming undone. It's oily. Unclean. Her make-up is smeared.

> *Silence.*

Your father wants you to live with him

> *Beat.*

I love you both so much

> *Beat.*

This room is a pigsty

So clean it up

Make it clean

For Mummy

Please

> …

She leaves.

6

A beat. JASPER and LEON look at each other.

JASPER: WE'RE GONNA LIVE AT THE MANSION WITH DAD!!!

LEON: Make your bed, Jasper.

LEON starts to clean the room.

JASPER: I've always wanted to live in a mansion! I was BORN to live in a mansion!

LEON: Calm your farm, Jasper. We have to clean up first.

JASPER: But when we do, I'm gonna jump off the balcony and onto a trampoline and then into the pool. Off the balcony … onto the trampoline … and into the pool. Hey, do you reckon Mum will come and live at the mansion too?

LEON: I doubt it. I think her and "Dad's friend" are, like, arch-enemies.

JASPER: What's an arch-enemy?

LEON: It's someone's worst enemy ever in the history of the world. That's what "Dad's friend" is to Mum.

JASPER: What does "" that mean? *(Makes the quotation mark sign.)*

LEON: It means Bunny Ears.

JASPER: Why does she have bunny ears?

LEON: Just clean up, Jasper.

They keep cleaning. (Feel free to say the names of Pooface, Theophilus or Trevor (the toys) as you pack them away, or even better – make up your own names) This sequence should take quite awhile.

JASPER: I hope she doesn't hate us so that we can live in her mansion.

LEON: You don't even like her.

JASPER: I know, but I still want her mansion. I wanna take over her kingdom. And her trampoline. Overthrow her.

LEON: She doesn't like you either.

JASPER: Correction. She doesn't like us.

LEON: No, just you. She thinks I'm OK.

JASPER: Maybe we should kill her. Like … eat heaps of beans and then sneak into her bedroom and fart in a pillow case and then put it over her head and watch her suffocate on our fart gas.

LEON: I don't think that would work.

JASPER: I reckon if I ate enough beans it would.

LEON: You don't even like beans.

JASPER: It's a sacrifice I'm willing to make.

LEON: If you killed "Dad's friend", you'd go to jail and then you wouldn't get your mansion. And trust me, Jasper, I reckon you wouldn't last five minutes in jail.

JASPER: I think you're just trying to scare me. I think I'll just hatch a plan and then we'll be famous for killing Mum's arch-enemesis and I can jump off the balcony onto the trampoline and into the pool. Hey, how can you tell if a shark is alive or dead?

LEON: How?

JASPER: Stab it.

A beat.

LEON: That's lame.

JASPER: I spent hours coming up with that one.

Silence.

They keep cleaning.

JASPER: Do you think she's pretty?

LEON: Who?

JASPER: "Dad's friend".

LEON: I dunno.

JASPER: She wears lots of make-up.

LEON: Who cares?

JASPER: I reckon it makes her look weird. She looks like this …

JASPER impersonates Dad's friend.

LEON: She doesn't look that bad.

JASPER: She does. She looks like a chicken in lipstick.

He struts a little more like a chicken in lipstick, his chest pushed out, his mouth pouting.

LEON: She looks younger than Mum. In fact, don't tell Mum I said this, but I think she looks nicer than Mum.

They get to the beds and start to make them, singing The Blue Danube as they do. (The original cast decided on The Blue Danube, but feel free to pick your own song here.)

JASPER: You know what I reckon?

LEON: What?

JASPER: You LOVE her.

LEON: What? Who?

JASPER: "Dad's friend". You totally LOVE her. You think she's pretty.

LEON: I do not!

JASPER: You don't want to kill her with fart gas. That's a dead giveaway.

LEON: You're the one who keeps talking about going to live with her.

JASPER: I saw the way you looked at her when we met her that time. You looked like this …

He demonstrates by wrapping his arms around his torso and wriggling.

LEON: You're an idiot. I hate her.

JASPER: Leon loves "Dad's friend"! Leon loves "Dad's friend"!

He calls to the door.

MUM! Leon loves "Dad's friend"!

LEON: Shut up! I do not!

JASPER: You want to marry her! You want to steal her off Dad and marry her! And then I'd be your stepson! YUCK!

(Feel free to overlap your dialogue here.)

LEON: Shut up, Jasper!

JASPER: You LOVE her! Like a teenager!!!

LEON: SHUT UP!

JASPER: YOU LOVE "DAD'S FRIEND"!

LEON is furious. He fights JASPER the best he can. He wraps JASPER up in a sheet, but JASPER keeps teasing him and making kissy noises. LEON is very angry and very upset. He shoves JASPER, wrapped in the sheet, under the bed.

LEON: The bed is YOUR space!

He indicates the bed.

And this is MY space!

He indicates the rest of the room.

Stay in your own territory or you die.

7

LEON lays on his own bed. He gets a yellow woollen jumper out from behind the dresser and holds it close. He inhales it.

Silence.

Weird snorting from underneath JASPER's bed.

JASPER: Uh-oh.

LEON ignores him.

I said UH-OH!

LEON ignores his brother again.

Nosebleed.

LEON ignores him.

Leon! My nose is bleeding!

LEON ignores him. JASPER climbs out from under the bed. His nose is bleeding.

He goes to step over his 'line'.

LEON: No!

JASPER stands with a bleeding nose.

JASPER: I have a blood nose!

LEON: You gave that to yourself.

JASPER: Did not.

LEON: You did that snorting thing.

JASPER: Did not.

He goes to step over the line again.

LEON: No!

JASPER notices the jumper.

JASPER: What's that?

LEON tries to hide the jumper.

LEON: Nothing.

JASPER: That's …

He goes to step over the line.

LEON: No!

JASPER steps back.

JASPER: That's Dad's jumper!

LEON: So?

JASPER: Where did you get it?

LEON: Just leave it, Jasper.

JASPER: I thought all his stuff was gone.

LEON: Well, you thought wrong.

JASPER: Can I have a hold?

He goes to step over the line.

LEON: No! Back!

JASPER steps back.

No.

JASPER: I just want to hold it.

LEON: Well, what you want and what you're gonna get are two different things.

JASPER: I'll tell Mum.

LEON: No you won't.

JASPER: I'll tell Mum you've got Dad's jumper. She'll be SO angry.

LEON: You say anything and you're dead.

JASPER goes to step off the bed again.

LEON stops him furiously.

LEON: NO!

JASPER looks frustrated. Then – a lightbulb moment. He concentrates hard then waves his hand like a magician.

JASPER: Oogedy-boogedy-bee – Jasper be free.

He steps over the line. He runs for the jumper again.

LEON: I said get back!

JASPER: I used magic and now I'm free. Deal with it.

JASPER grabs the jumper. LEON grabs the jumper too. A tug of war. A chase. Both desperate to gain control of Jason's jumper. JASPER puts his bloody nose near the jumper threateningly.

JASPER: Drop it or I'll bleed on it.

LEON: Jasper!

JASPER: I will!

LEON drops the jumper. He backs off. JASPER is triumphant.

JASPER: Right. Let's negotiate terms. You can have Dad's jumper if you give me something in return.

LEON: OK. What. What do you want?

JASPER: Your guns.

A beat. LEON considers.

LEON: Fine. Take it.

JASPER: GunS.

LEON: You can't have them both. You need me to be your enemy and shoot you.

JASPER: When I want to have a fight, I'll loan you the gun and you can give it back when the battle's over.

LEON gives JASPER both his guns.

JASPER: And the ammo.

LEON hands over the ammo.

And I want your fish.

LEON: But that's –

JASPER: I want Cornelius. Do you want Dad's jumper or not?

He holds the jumper to his nose again. LEON sighs. He walks over to the fish tank. Speaks to Cornelius.

LEON: Cornelius, I hereby declare you now belong to Jasper.

JASPER: Yes!

He turns back to JASPER.

LEON: Happy?

JASPER is. Very. He hands back the jumper.

Shake on it?

JASPER holds out his hand. So does LEON. LEON's fingers are crossed.

Oh no, Jasper! Look at that! See? My fingers were crossed the whole entire time! That means everything that just happened was completely false! You lost! Sorry.

JASPER: That's not fair!

LEON: Fingers crossed. You lose. That's the law. *(Beat.)* And if you dare try and tell Mum about the jumper again, I'm gonna call the Shadow Monster and get it to visit you tonight.

JASPER looks stunned.

JASPER: You wouldn't dare.

LEON: I would.

JASPER: You can't call anyway. The phone's in the quiet room.

LEON: Let's just say the Shadow Monster and I have other methods of communication.

JASPER: Facebook?

LEON: Just know that I can call upon the Shadow Monster at any time. Without you even knowing. It might even be here right now. So be careful.

LEON puts on his headphones and closes his eyes as he listens to the music.

JASPER looks around the room, terrified.

Really, really scared.

He crosses his legs. He needs to wee.

8

MEDEA enters.

JASPER screams and hides – he thinks she's the Shadow Monster.

MEDEA holds a beautifully wrapped present.

She places it on JASPER's bed.

JASPER's eyes pop as he comes out from his hiding spot.

JASPER: Is that for me?!

MEDEA: No.

JASPER is extremely disappointed.

Oh, darling, it's even better than being FOR you. It's FROM you.

LEON: Who's it for?

MEDEA: It's for your Dad's friend.

LEON and JASPER are confused.

JASPER: I thought she was your arch-enemesis.

MEDEA beams.

MEDEA: What? No! I think she's wonderful. She's a very special lady. Very pretty and very rich, from a good family. And she loves you. Not as much as I love you. But she does. Do you know that?

LEON rather likes this fact.

LEON: Really?

MEDEA: Really. In fact, Dad's friend loves you both so much that now **SHE** has decided she wants you to live in the mansion with her and Daddy. How about that, huh?

JASPER: Awesome! Off the balcony, onto the trampoline, into the pool!

A beat.

LEON: What about you, Mum?

MEDEA: Well, now Mummy has to take a trip back to her own home.

LEON: But you hate your own home, Mum.

JASPER: Granddad's angry with you.

LEON: Everyone is.

JASPER: What did you do wrong, Mum? Was it a cigarette?

MEDEA: I just fell in love, darling. That's all. Love can make you do strange things sometimes. So I have to go home. But it won't be for long. I promise. So don't you worry, because now Dad's friend has promised to take you into her mansion while I'm away. Insisted, in fact. Isn't that nice? That's why I've made her a very special present. To say thank you for being so kind to my little boys.

JASPER: What kind of present? Can we see it?

MEDEA: No! It's a grown-up present. From one woman to another. Do you think it looks nice?

The boys shrug.

I tell you what – how about you write a card for Dad's Friend?

The boys are reluctant.

Your handwriting has been improving so much lately. And your spelling. Let's show off a little, hey?

LEON: Mum, if we write the card can we go outside afterwards?

MEDEA: Of course, my love. Of course.

The boys hurry to the toy box and get out paper and markers. They sit down to write the letter. LEON has the marker.

LEON: I don't know how to start. I've never written to a girl before.

JASPER: Start with … "My dearest Dad's friend …"

LEON: 'My dearest'?

JASPER: It's polite. Girls like polite things. Don't they, Mum?

MEDEA: They certainly do.

LEON writes.

LEON: "My dearest Dad's friend …"

JASPER: Don't forget to put the bunny ears.

LEON does.

LEON: "Dad's ... friend."

JASPER: "Hope you like the present ..."

LEON writes.

Now ask her how high her balcony is, how deep her pool is and if she has a trampoline.

LEON: Jasper, we can find that stuff out when we move in.

JASPER: And ask her if we can bring our stars and stick them on the walls. I'm not going anywhere without my stars.

LEON: Jasper –

JASPER: And ask her where our spots will be at the table. I like to sit next to Mum, so she better make sure Mum's invited to dinner every night. Tell her.

MEDEA: Yes. Tell her that.

JASPER: And tell her she looks like a chicken with lips.

MEDEA laughs at this. She laughs and laughs and laughs. JASPER loves that she's laughing. He impersonates Dad's friend. A chicken with lips. So does MEDEA. JASPER does another, more exaggerated impersonation. MEDEA loves it.

LEON looks frustrated.

LEON: How about just "To 'Dad's friend' from Jasper and Leon."

MEDEA settles down.

MEDEA: Thank you, darling. It's perfect. Just perfect.

She puts the card with the gift, carefully. She kisses both the boys then walks to the door.

JASPER: Mum ... you smell funny.

MEDEA: Do I? Do I?

LEON: You smell like chemicals.

MEDEA sniffs her hands.

MEDEA: I do a bit, don't I? Damn.

LEON: Mum, what's in the present?

MEDEA: It's a secret. Shhh.

She goes to the door.

LEON: Can we please come /out now?

MEDEA: Soon. Your Daddy will be coming to get you soon. Any minute! Are you excited? I am!

She shuts the door.

Silence.

Nothing.

The boys just stare at the door.

Just as they're turning away ...

MEDEA opens it again.

MEDEA: Boys. Sometimes when I look at you I get so scared.

I see everything coming, you see and ...

A long silence. She stares at them. They stare back. She sniffs her hand.

And I love you.

I love you both.

I scream it into my pillow every night how much I love you. I scream so hard to the universe that I'll bet there's cavemen from millions of years ago that stop what they're doing and say, "Did you hear that?" And I scream so hard that there are robots thousands of years from now that say "Listen. That was a mother who loves her children more than anything in the history of the universe."

But just in case the universe and everyone that's been here and everyone that's coming to it doesn't hear me scream it, I want you to know that.

Please know that.

I love you. So much. Infinitely.

My boys.

And everything I do is because of that.

She leaves.

9

JASPER shakes his head at what his mum has just said.

JASPER: She is so dumb.

LEON: She's not dumb. Don't say that.

JASPER: Well, she is. Cavemen didn't speak English, Leon. They spoke Neanderthal.

LEON: I don't think that's the moral of the story.

JASPER: And robots don't have feelings so they don't know what love is.

LEON: She didn't mean it like that.

JASPER: Well … she's just weird.

Silence. LEON doodles on the paper.

What do you reckon is inside the present? A giant man-eating panda?

LEON: I think it's soap.

JASPER: Why would you get someone soap? You can just buy that.

LEON: Yeah, but this way you get it for free.

A beat. JASPER has another lightbulb moment.

JASPER: Wait, Dad's coming! We have to get our swords! We have to show him we've been practising! Quick. He's on his way. Any minute! Are you excited? I am!

They run to the toy box and get out two wooden swords.

LEON: En guarde.

JASPER: On guard!

LEON: Form.

JASPER adjusts his sword-fighting form, but gets too close to LEON.

LEON: Measure.

JASPER steps back a little.

Jasper, you have to go slow, remember? Dad said we have to go as slow as possible until he comes back.

JASPER: But we've been going slow for ages.

LEON: They're the rules of sword fighting. Go slow until Dad says go fast.

JASPER looks peeved.

Now, eyes.

JASPER looks LEON in the eye.

Cue.

JASPER prepares.

Extend.

JASPER extends his arm.

Thrust.

JASPER thrusts.

LEON performs a seconde.

Two!

LEON performs another seconde.

Riposte!

They part swords.

Riposte!

Back to seconde.

Bind and throw!

LEON blocks JASPER's sword and pushes him away. He falls on his hands on LEON's bed. He turns and swings an overarm joust at LEON.

JASPER: And cut to the head!

LEON: EYES! Jasper, remember, you always have to look me in the eye. Position two.

They go to position two, this time with LEON in front of his bed and JASPER in front of his own bed.

En guarde.

Form.

LEON suddenly begins fighting swiftly, much to JASPER's surprise.

And reprise! Septime! Quinte! Seconde!

And parry! Parry! Parry! Parry!

JASPER is desperate.

JASPER: RIPOSTE!

JASPER thrusts toward LEON. LEON ducks away from JASPER's sword and touches his own sword on JASPER's back.

LEON: TOUCHE! And the crowd goes wild! Thank you! Thank you!

JASPER stands awkwardly, his legs crossed tightly.

JASPER: That wasn't Dad's fight.

LEON: Salut! Salut!

LEON bows triumphantly.

The crowd are on their feet, but none are so proud as Leon's father Jason, who can only sit, his legs like jelly, with tears in his eyes, as he watches his first-born son claim glory.

The daydream dissipates.

LEON checks the door. Still locked.

LEON turns and sees his brother is laying on the bed, beneath the duvet.

LEON: You OK?

Jasper?

Nothing.

Nincompoop?

Nothing.

It's only a game.

Don't get upset.

Silence.

Then, softly from beneath his duvet …

JASPER: I wet my pants.

LEON: What?

JASPER: I tried to hold on but a little bit trickled out.

LEON: Gross. I can smell it.

JASPER: I was bursting.

LEON: It stinks.

JASPER: Of course it stinks! It's urine! Now I'm itchy.

LEON: You've got to learn to hold on to your fluids, Jasper. Honestly, you're always dripping from one end or the other. It's completely embarrassing.

Silence.

JASPER starts to weep softly.

See?! Drip, drip drip! Piss, piss, piss! Drip, drip drip!

JASPER cries more.

A long moment. LEON softens a little.

Jasper, don't cry.

JASPER cries even more.

Jasp. It doesn't matter.

Jasper …

JASPER cries.

Then, quietly.

JASPER: I'm so sick of being small.

LEON: You're not that small. There's smaller things than you. Insects. Amoebas.

JASPER: I'm the smallest person out of everyone I know.

LEON: You'll get bigger. You will. I did.

JASPER: No matter how big I get, you'll always win the sword fights.

Silence. LEON goes to his brother.

LEON: There's more to life than sword fights, Jasper. You do other things much better than me.

JASPER: Like what?

LEON: Like the animal game. You know animals that I've never even heard of. Like narwhals. You're so smart like that.

JASPER: Whatever.

Silence.

LEON: And dancing. You're such a great dancer.

Silence.

JASPER: I am a pretty good dancer.

Silence.

LEON: And you can sing really well. Sing that song for me that I like.

A beat. JASPER grabs a ukelele by the bed. He stands on his bed, his pants wet with urine, and sings a song. (The original cast chose to sing 'Octopus's Garden', but feel free to choose your own to match the moment.)

They sing a few lines from Octopus's Garden. His smile disappears. He scratches his wet legs and lays back on the bed, miserably.

A beat.

LEON gets a T-shirt and pyjama bottoms out of his drawer.

LEON: Get changed.

JASPER goes to take off his pants then looks embarrassed. He climbs under his covers. He wriggles into his fresh clothes – privately and out of view of anyone else. LEON doesn't watch. He turns around respectfully.

LEON: You need any help?

JASPER: I'm fine.

He keeps getting dressed. He holds out his wet pants and undies from beneath the duvet. LEON takes them. (Careful – they're covered in wee!)

LEON puts the wet clothes underneath JASPER's mattress.

JASPER is dressed. He covers the wet patch on his mattress with the duvet and lays down again.

JASPER: No wonder Dad hasn't been to visit for ages. Not even for my birthday. I embarrass him. I can't even hold my wee in.

LEON: That's not true. Dad loves you. He loves both of us.

JASPER: Then where is he?

LEON: He's coming. Dad's friend will love the present and then he'll come and get us and we'll all move into the mansion and everything's going to be fine.

Silence.

And even if things aren't fine, you know what? The best thing about having a big brother is that big brothers have a responsibility to their little brothers to take care of them always. Forever. So even when we're really old – like, in our thirties – I'll still take care of you. Because I'll always, always be your big brother. And so it's always, always my job to take care of you. Because I love you. And I love being your big brother.

LEON gets a luminescent star out of his bedside drawer.

Here. Have a star.

JASPER: Really?

LEON: Add it to the galaxy.

JASPER: Awesome!

JASPER sticks the star amongst the others on the wall. He names his new star.

Jasperellis Borealis.

LEON turns off the light.

The stage is plunged into blackness, but a huge galaxy of stars is revealed across the space.

They both lay under the illuminated stars.

Their voices float out from the dark.

JASPER: Leon, when you look up at the stars, do you think you're on earth or on another planet?

LEON: Neither. I think I'm just floating. Just floating through space and time.

JASPER: Like an astronaut?

LEON: Kind of. But without the suit. Just me. Like this.

JASPER: And what else?

LEON: And it's quiet. And still. And peaceful. And I just … give in to it all. Because it's so much bigger than me.

You know that, Jasper? You may think you're really little, but really, we're all really, really little.

Even Dad.

We're just … specks. Specks of specks. And that may sound scary, but it's not, really.

It's kind of comforting.

We're all tiny, all floating, all … powerless.

Yeah. That's what it is. We're completely powerless.
To everything.

Silence.

LEON stares at the stars. He sings softly.

JASPER joins in …

10

A long, long, long moment in the dark room.

Then …

A shadow at the door.

The door opens.

A shadow falls across the boys.

MEDEA.

She holds two glasses of green cordial.

JASPER turns on his bedside lamp and MEDEA is caught in its glare.

LEON: Mum? Did you send the present to Dad's friend?

Silence.

JASPER: Mum? Did you?

MEDEA smiles.

Speaks softly.

MEDEA: I did. I really, really did. We did it.

The boys watch her for a while.

LEON: So … did she like it?

JASPER: What WAS it? Was it soap?

MEDEA: She's gone.

Silence.

LEON: What?

MEDEA: She's 'gone'.

Silence.

JASPER: Where?

MEDEA: I don't know.

Beat. LEON and MEDEA stare at each other.

JASPER: Mum …

MEDEA: Yes, darling?

JASPER: I weed myself a bit.

MEDEA: Darling, did you?

JASPER: I couldn't hold my legs together any more.

MEDEA: Oh, darling.

She looks stunned. A moment of realisation.

I'm sorry. I'm so sorry. i'm sorry i'm sorry.

JASPER: It's OK. Leon got me some fresh pants.

MEDEA: Oh. And undies?

JASPER: Yes.

Pause.

MEDEA: Here. A special drink.

JASPER: Cordial? Now?

MEDEA: Yes.

She hands them the glasses.

The boys drink as they watch MEDEA.

LEON: Why did she go?

MEDEA: What?

LEON: Dad's friend. Why did she 'go'?

JASPER: Didn't she like the present? Our card?

MEDEA: No. She didn't like it. It was a big surprise for her. But she didn't like it. And now she's 'gone' and we're in a bit of trouble. Keep drinking.

LEON: Has Dad 'gone' with her?

MEDEA: No. No, Daddy's still at the mansion.

JASPER: Is he still coming to pick me and Leon up?

MEDEA: Of course! Any minute. He'll be coming for all of us. Drink up.

LEON: All of us? I thought you were going back to your old home.

MEDEA: Not anymore. Not back there.

JASPER: But are we still going to live in the mansion?

MEDEA: Somewhere even better.

JASPER: Even better than the mansion? Oh my stars! What's even better than the mansion?!

MEDEA: It's a secret. Daddy will come soon.

LEON: Is he angry with us?

They finish their drinks.

MEDEA: Finished? Good. Now come on. Up.

She whips back their bed covers. The boys still aren't convinced. Something feels funny in their tummies.

LEON: What? No. Mum ... we're looking at the stars.

MEDEA: Get up.

LEON: And Jasper had a blood nose.

JASPER: And we haven't had dinner.

MEDEA: Please, darlings. Get up.

LEON: It's dark. I'm tired. We can wait till the morning, can't we?

JASPER: And we haven't had dessert.

MEDEA: Please –

LEON: Mum, maybe we should just –

MEDEA: Look, it doesn't matter!

Beat. MEDEA softens.

Nothing matters. Nothing means anything anymore. Get up. Please.

They do.

Come here. I want to make you look nice for Daddy.

They walk to her. They seem tired.

MEDEA undresses the boys.

She takes off their jumpers.

Then their shirts.

Then their sneakers.

Then their trousers.

They are now in just their underpants.

They are uncomfortable. This is weird.

MEDEA leaves.

LEON grins at his little brother's tiny frame.

LEON: Nice legs.

JASPER: Shut up. You can talk.

LEON: I have Dad's legs. You have Mum's. That means you have lady's legs.

JASPER: I do not. They're small but muscular.

LEON: Not from up here, they're not.

MEDEA re-enters with two small suits on hangers, as well as two pairs of shoes and socks.

She starts to redress them in these clothes.

LEON tries to do it himself.

MEDEA: Let me do it.

He doesn't let her.

MEDEA focuses her attention on JASPER instead.

A long silence as they dress.

Then ... LEON whispers.

LEON: Narwhal.

JASPER: Lemming.

LEON: What's a lemming?

JASPER: Animals that jump off cliffs.

LEON: Why would they jump off a cliff?

JASPER: Cos they followed the Pied Piper.

LEON: That's a fairy tale. Lemmings aren't real.

JASPER: They are! Mum, are lemmings real? Mum?

MEDEA is still dressing the boys.

MEDEA: Yes.

JASPER: Ha! See? Lemming. G.

LEON: G. Gorilla.

JASPER: Anaconda.

LEON: Alligator.

JASPER: Rrrr ... rrrr ... reptile.

LEON: That's not a specific animal.

JASPER: It just has to be an animal. A reptile is an animal, isn't it, Mum?

MEDEA: Yes.

LEON: OK. Reptile. E. Elephant seal.

JASPER: Llll ... ocust.

LEON: Tit.

JASPER: Um-ah! Mum! Leon said t-i-t.

LEON: What?! It's a bird, retard! A tit is a bird, isn't it, Mum?

MEDEA: Yes.

JASPER: Well, I'm not going to say it because it's disgusting. T-I-T. T … T … Terradactyl.

LEON: Lioness.

JASPER: Slug.

LEON: German Shepherd.

JASPER: Drake.

LEON: What's a drake?

JASPER: It's a male duck.

LEON: A male duck? Really? Then what's a female duck called?

JASPER: A female duck's just a duck. The male duck gets a special name because he's the male.

LEON: I've never heard of it.

JASPER: Fine. Dog.

LEON: G … r … iffin. Griffin.

JASPER: Doesn't exist.

LEON: Does so. Dad told me. He saw one once. Didn't he, Mum?

MEDEA: Yes.

LEON: See! Told you. On his travels.

JASPER: I'm sure they don't exist. Mum, did he really see a Griffin? Mum?

MEDEA: Yes.

JASPER: Argh. Griffin. Nnnnnn … Nin … com … poop … I feel funny.

> *MEDEA stops putting on JASPER's shoes momentarily and stares at JASPER as he rubs his eyes. LEON is tired too. JASPER keeps playing the game.*

Um … nits.

LEON: Nits?

JASPER: Yeah. So … nit.

LEON: Nit?

JASPER: Nits. Is it nit or nits?

LEON: I dunno. You can have nits, so I guess one would be a nit.

JASPER: Mum, is there such thing as a nit?

MEDEA: Yes.

JASPER: Awesome. Nit.

They are dressed. MEDEA combs their hair. Cleans their faces. They respond as any self-respecting young man would. As she does … The boys yawn and play on.

LEON: Nit. T … Tasmanian devil.

JASPER: Loris.

LEON: Slow loris.

JASPER: Salamander.

LEON: What's that?

JASPER: It's a really wet lizard.

LEON: Did you make that up?

JASPER: No.

LEON: Cross your heart, hope to die?

JASPER crosses his heart.

OK. What does it end in? A?

JASPER: Um … not sure. A, I think. Mum, does 'salamander' end in A?

MEDEA: Yes.

LEON: Ok. A … Aardvark.

JASPER: Kangaroo.

LEON: Opossum.

JASPER: Maggot.

LEON: Termite.

JASPER: Earthworm.

LEON: Mammoth.

JASPER: Extinct!

LEON: It doesn't matter! It doesn't matter if they're dead. They used to be alive. Their bones are still getting dug up. They were here. They existed. Didn't they, Mum?

MEDEA is silent. She makes them stand side by side.

Mum, didn't they?

MEDEA is silent.

Mum?

MEDEA stares at them in their little suits.

MEDEA: There.

Finally, they stand before her. Dressed, cleaned, ready to go. And very, very sleepy.

JASPER: I'm tired.

MEDEA: Then lay down.

LEON: I thought you wanted us up.

MEDEA: Now I want you to lay down, darling.

LEON: But we just got dressed.

MEDEA: Come on. I'll lay down with you and we'll wait for Daddy.

As they lay down, LEON gets out his Golden Fleece jumper.

Is that … Where did you get that?

LEON: Dad gave it to me.

MEDEA: I didn't realise you had that.

LEON: Can I keep it?

A beat.

MEDEA: Yes.

MEDEA lays back with her boys.

I love every single bit of you. Every tiny particle of you.

To JASPER:

You, precious stone. I love your breath. Your breath has always been delicious. It's better than chocolate. It's better than strawberry marshmallows, your breath.

To LEON:

And you, brave heart. I love your freckles. I love that you are covered in freckles. You even have freckles on your eyelids. I love that.

To JASPER:

And you, funny munchkin. I love the way you call out for me when you have a bad dream. When the Shadow Monster visits you in your sleep and I scoop you up and you cling to my neck like a little monkey.

To LEON:

And you, my big beautiful boy. I love watching you play your sports. You're getting so big and tall and strong and I can see your new muscles. You're so like your father, my handsome one. So like your father. I love you so much.

To both of them.

And I love watching you sleep, my loves. Sometimes I get so close to you when you're sleeping that I can see your hearts beating beneath your pyjamas.

LEON drops the Golden Fleece jumper and snuggles into his Mum.

I love your feet. I love your tummy rumbles when you're hungry. I love the way you chew your straw. I love the jokes you invent. I love the way you dance in your socks. I love your little farts. I love washing your clothes and seeing the remnants of your day spilled on them. I love your hair. Oh, how I love your hair. I love that I was the first one to run my fingers through it. I was the first. I love your blood. I love you more than anyone has ever loved anything. My beautiful sons of the daughter of the Sun. My ones. My loves. My only loves.

LEON and JASPER are dead.

Their head fall back, their mouths gape, but MEDEA doesn't let them go.

She doesn't let them go.

She screams silently, but doesn't let them go.

The fish swim.

MEDEA looks to the door expectantly, clutching the corpses of JASPER and LEON.

The lights dim.

The lights dim.

The lights dim until all that's left are the glowing stars.

END.